MOSCOW

Photographs by Nikolai Rakhmanov

MOSCOW

Photographs by
NIKOLAI PAKHMANOV

Moscow
Interbook Business Publishers
2006

Interbook Business Publishers project

Text by
ALEKSANDR SHPIKALOV

Designed by
ALEKSEY VISHTALYUK

Translated from the Russian by
OLEG GLEBOV

Printed by Gorenjski Tisk, Slovenia

ISBN 5-89164-085-6

© Рахманов Н.Н., фотографии, 2006
© Шпикалов А.Г., текст, 2006
© Глебов О.А., перевод на английский язык, 2006
© Оформление. ЗАО «Интербук-бизнес», 2006

Moscow is not just a speechless pile of stones,
symmetrically arranged—No! It has a soul
of its own, a life of its own... Each of its stones bears
an inscription carved by the Time...

MIKHAIL LERMONTOV

In central Russia there quietly flows a river known as Moskva, the name of legends and historical memories. It was the picturesque banks of the Moskva river that had attracted Prince Yury Dolgoruky and gave the name to the capital of the future vast state.

The "birth certificate" of Moscow is the Ipatievskaya chronicle which contains a record of 1147 with the passage describing how Prince Yury (George) Dolgoruky invited his relative and ally Prince Svyatoslav to the new city where the guest was "splendidly feasted".

A ten-year older record in the Tverskaya chronicle confirms the existence of the city saying: "Prince Yury founded the city of Moscow at the confluence of the Neglinnaya river and the Moskva river." The Prince of Suzdal and Grand Duke of Kiev, Prince Yury, had the great honor of founding the capital of Russia.

In the 1270s Moscow become the center of a principality and Prince Ivan Kalita (the Moneybag) established it as the real capital of the Vladimir-Suzdal Russia. The old stockade on the steep Kremlin hill could not cope with the new dangers befalling the chief city of the principality. In 1339 Ivan Kalita erected a new "fort of oak-wood" which was significantly extended in the northern and eastern directions. As can be seen from the Voskresenskaya chronicle from 1331 the fort was known as the Kremlin. The first cathedrals made of white stone were rising above the wooden buildings as first tokens of the future magnificence of the Russian capital.

The oak-wood Kremlin of Ivan Kalita did not survive for long. In 1365 the Kremlin and the surrounding outskirts beyond the river burned out in the greatest of the fifty-odd fires that regularly happened in Moscow in the 12th—15th centuries. In two years Prince Dmitry Donskoy caused a grand fortress to be built with towers and walls of white stone. The 2 000-meter-long walls surrounded almost the entire area of what is now the contemporary Kremlin. That was the structure that gave the name of "white-stone" to all major Moscow developments.

The Tatar horde led by Khan Tokhtamysh besieged the Kremlin in 1382. The strong stone walls and the bravery of the Moscow warriors failed to save Moscow from destruction. The so-called Tokhtamysh devastation was bitterly remembered by Muscovites for at least two centuries.

In the late 15th century the tsar Ivan III proclaimed himself the "tsar of all Russia". Moscow became the capital of the centralized Russian state. Ivan III started to implement a remarkably wide construction program. He caused practically the entire Kremlin to be rebuilt and now it has essentially the same character as was created by Ivan III.

At the beginning of the reign of Ivan IV the Terrible a great fire broke down in June 1547 which was followed by a serious popular unrest. The windy weather fanned up the fire throughout the city; in ten hours the city was obliterated and thousands of men, women and children died from suffocation with smoke and burns. Almost the entire Moscow population was left homeless. The tsar himself escaped from the fire to the Vorobievo village on the Moskva River bank.

Fires were repeated from one year to another, from one century to another... The city had perished but then was resurrected again proudly standing in the Russian plains at the crossroads of the trade routes.

The Russian Middle Ages was the time when great many nameless genius craftsmen were toiling, when they built, clothed, fed, armed and adorned Moscow. They were ceaselessly cutting lumber, casting metal, building boats, sewing jerkins and trousers, and minting coins with "the horse rider with a spear" which was to become the future emblem of the city. The most visible results of their labors were the new cathedrals and palaces in the Moscow streets. We do not know the names of most of them. However, the names of the blacksmiths, icon painters, potters, figure-casters, tanners, carpenters, jewelers, armorers, and other craftsmen remained forever in the names of the Moscow streets, lanes, and quarters.

The fairy-tale image of the medieval Moscow invariably impressed numerous foreign visitors. For instance, the French nobleman Astolphe de Cuistine who had been invited to Russia by the Emperor Nikolai I wrote, "The multitude of the church domes, spires and elaborate turrets was sparkling in the sun over the dust clouds rising from the road... Try to imagine a picture that cannot be represented with paints... It is a veritable phantasmagoria that makes Moscow a unique city, there is nothing like

environment. Moscow is a city of an entirely different character. Its beauty is a complex phenomenon, it is unfolding gradually like an intricate theater performance packed with dramatic events. The ultimate richness and variety of its image are born from the overlays of different cultural impacts generated throughout its long history. The architectural panorama of Moscow is extremely mixed as it reflects the passage of time over the city. The utter incongruity of the past and the ongoing transformations is sometimes emphasized by the appearance of adjacent structures of inconsistent sizes and architectonic styles built in different periods.

By the early 17th century Moscow had acquired a surprisingly integral image. The Kremlin remained the architectural center of the city. The squat towers and the cathedral domes glittering behind the Kremlin walls produced a much sterner and menacing impression than the Kremlin ensemble that we know now. The subsequent class of the imposing architectural ensembles consisted of the large monasteries and nunneries: the Alekseevsky, Georgievsky, Nikitsky, Zlatoustovsky, Ivanovsky, and other. The architectural ensembles of each monastery were looking as if they were scaled-down copies of the Kremlin ensemble. Other areas of the city were spatially arranged through the same model. The groups of ordinary everyday buildings were plain and modest in appearance. The more impressive against their background were the unique structures such as cathedrals and palaces.

Before the 17th century the city still lacked that wide variety of the verticals that is its distinguishing feature in our days. The Uspensky Cathedral, which was the tallest building in Moscow, was only 45 meters high. The 60-meter high Saint Basil Cathedral was the next tallest building. Finally, in 1600 the Ivan the Great tower was raised up to the 81-meter mark.

The second half of the 17th century was a prosperous period in the Moscow history. The city economy was growing and the city was expanding. The Kremlin had lost its defensive function and its architectural ensemble was continually being upgraded as befitted the seat of the supreme state authority.

The French invasion of 1812 was a devastating blow for Moscow, which was no longer the capital city of the Russian Empire but preserved rich historical traditions. The Russian society was badly struck by the momentous transformation of their cozy hospitable Moscow into the battlefront area. Till the last moment before the French troops entered Moscow the Russian patriots were still hoping to engage them in the final fight at the "ancient Kremlin gate". An eyewitness of the French invasion and the subsequent firestorm wrote, "The glory of

White-stone Kremlin at the time of Dmitry Donskoy. Reconstructed by A.M. Vasnetsov. 1922

View of the Kremlin from the Tainitskaya Tower. Fragment of the panorama. Lithograph by F. Benois and Obrain after a sketch by Indeitsev. The 1850s

it in Europe..." A hundred years later Knut Hamsun, a Nobel Prize winning Norwegian novelist, who had traveled practically all over the globe admitted, "Moscow is something from a fairly tale... I have visited four of the five continents but I had seen nothing like the Moscow Kremlin... A veritable sea of beauty opens to one's eyes from the Kremlin. I could never have imagined that such a city could exist on the Earth: everything around you is flashing from the red and golden domes and spires. The golden mass in combination with the deep blue of the sky is much more impressive than any of my dreams."

There exist cities, which have been build according to a rigorous plan, they are exhibiting an enticing harmony of the overall image, a regular sequence of marble façades or granite embankments. Venice and Saint Petersburg are such cities, which display the utmost artistic harmony of the urban

Moscow is being burned down to ashes, its holy churches, its huge palaces, its historical landmarks are being devastated." Many Muscovites were desperate and thinking that no hope remained for restoring the former glory of the city. However, in the late 1812 Moscow seemed one busy great construction site. More than 8500 buildings were renovated, new squares and neighborhoods were laid out. The central part of Moscow was significantly reconstructed. The Red Square was cleaned and reserved for holding ceremonial parades and other official celebrations. The dirty evil-smelling water of the Neglinnaya River was passed through an underground tunnel on top of which the splendid Aleksandrovsky Park was laid out. Many other parks were renovated and created.

The city had rapidly grown after the devastating fire of 1812 but then remained almost untouched until the second half of the 19th century. The multi-volume history of Moscow by N. Vasilich says: "There remained the same irregular medley of the streets where the huge palaces of the aristocracy alternate with wooden huts and vacant plots overgrown with weeds, the same ancient churches with wide grassy churchyards, the same magnificent pile of the fairy-tale Kremlin looming over the city..." That was the end of the idyllically traditional period in the Moscow history.

It was back in 1835 that the great Russian poet and visionary Aleksandr Pushkin noted: "Moscow has lost its aristocratic glamour but is prospering in other respects as the industry is developing extremely fast owing to its encouragement and promotion." The economic and administrative reforms in the mid-19th century Russia gave an additional impetus to industrial development of Moscow. Numerous new industries were sprawling through the Moscow outskirts initially along the Moskva River and its tributary, the Yauza River, and in the late 19th century along the new railroads coming to Moscow. Densely populated housing estates sprang to life in the vicinity of the new industries. The old-fashioned tranquility of the Moscow life and style was harshly disturbed by the intrusion of new concepts and manners especially in the urban development trends.

The 20th-century artist and art historian Aleksandr Benois noted that the cultural centers in Moscow were no longer the domain of aristocracy, they have been taken over by the new class of industrialists and merchants. The textile manufacturer Tretyakov donated his immensely valuable art collection to the city of Moscow. The first higher educational institution for women and the new building of the Historical Museum in Moscow were financed by donations from rich merchants. The electric power stations were built in Moscow, many

new railroad stations were opened, and new electric street car lines were laid down. The rapid industrial and commercial development of Moscow was accompanied with the growth of poor neighborhoods around new plants and factories where working men and their families lived in the conditions of squalor and misery.

The central districts of Moscow were also affected in many adverse ways by the rapid economic development of the city. Many excellent architectural ensembles were destroyed by new buildings that suddenly emerged in their midst. As the demand for new housing and shops for the upscale tenants and more office space for rapidly growing companies and banks was rising fast the land value in central Moscow was going up at an even faster rate. The new buildings grew progressively taller and taller. In the early-19th century Moscow the three-story palaces and large detached town houses were standing above the clusters of single-story houses, often with a half-story at the top. The church domes and their bell-towers were major landmarks that could be seen from afar. The expansive vistas stretching before one's eyes as one moved along the banks of the Moskva River opened one after another the picturesque and intricate city outlines. It was the instinctive desire to preserve that type of a city outline that held the early Moscow developers from constructing buildings higher than three stories even when they were apartment blocks intended for rental income earning. However, in 1874 the first five-story apartment block was built on the Ilinka street. In the late 19th century most of the new apartment blocks in central Moscow within the Garden Ring had five stories or more. The first Russian "sky-scraper" apartment block of 11 stories was built on the Garden Ring in the early 20th century.

Moskvoretskaya street. Post card of the early 20th century

High-rise apartment block on Kotelnicheskaya embankment

New Arbat

the framework of the newly established social order. The Red Square was reconstructed to accommodate the massive granite structure of the Mausoleum where the embalmed body of the Communist revolution leader Vladimir Lenin was laid for public display.

The reconstruction work was started with the demolition of the Voskresenskie gate leading to the Red Square, the Iverskaya Chapel containing invaluable relics of the Russian Orthodox Church, and the ancient Kazansky Cathedral. Preparations were started for demolishing the Saint Basil Cathedral and the Historical Museum. The work on demolition of the architectural treasures of the past was carried out on an immense scale and much more was planned. Many magnificent buildings were destroyed in Moscow in the course of the reconstruction drive. The greatest of them was the Christ the Savior Cathedral near the Kremlin. Of course, the reconstruction drive entailed not only demolition work, there were many outstanding housing, sanitation, transportation issues and other problems of urban development to be resolved.

Five bridges across the Moskva River were built in the 1930s: Bolshoy Kamenny, Moskvoretsky, Krymsky, Ustinsky, and Bolshoy Krasnokholmsky. New housing estates were built. New experimental types of the housing, office and industrial architectural designs were developed and verified. Such unique novel types of buildings included the "Socialist-lifestyle housing" units, clubs for workers in the Stromynka street and the Lesnaya street, and the Planetarium.

The main streets in central Moscow were widened and generally renovated by the government orders starting in 1937 with the Gorky street leading from the Kremlin to the north-west.

The most fascinating development project was the construction of the underground railroad known as the Metro. The excavations made for the projects unearthed numerous archeological finds revealing secrets of the ancient Moscow. On May 15, 1935, the first Metro line was opened for the passenger traffic and many of the new Metro stations were architectural masterpieces in their own right, for instance, the "Mayakovskaya" station.

The World War II put a stop to implementation of the large-scale reconstruction projects but immediately after the Victory Day in May 1945 the bulldozers again went on crumbling the walls of the ancient buildings. New massive structures were erected in the Gorky street (now known under its original name Tverskaya street), Prospect Mira, and the Kutuzovsky Prospect. In the early 1950s at six construction sites in central Moscow and one on the steep bank of the Moskva River huge metal structures of the future Moscow skyscrapers had come

Massive office buildings emerged in the Kitai Gorod district around the Kremlin, which was the business center of Moscow. The architectural style of the so-called Business Center built in 1911 at the Varvarka street gate near the Kremlin was utterly alien to the Moscow traditions. The laws of capitalist development were relentlessly crushing the ancient architectural treasures beloved by old Muscovites.

After the Communist takeover Moscow was made the state capital in 1918.

The new government ordered a group of architects to work out plans for rebuilding Moscow in out. The new Moscow skyscrapers organically continued the tradition of the Moscow architecture and blended harmoniously into the eclectic architectural environment that was always typical of Moscow. The "wreath" of the verticals outlined by the new skyscrapers strikingly emphasized the historical center of Moscow.

At the same period the government started to expand fast the housing construction. The primary district for new housing was the south-west of the capital. Two major thoroughfares were built leading from the center to the new south-western housing estates. One is known as the Leninsky Prospect. The other, known as the Komsomolsky Prospect, led to the newly completed campus of the Moscow State University past the huge Luzhniki sports complex built in 1956 on the low Moskva River bank.

Since 1954 the government started a massive program of prefabricated housing construction. A few hundred thousand new apartments appeared in the former Moscow suburbs of Cheryemushki, Kuzminki, Izmailovo, Khoroshevo, Mnevniki and Fili. The architectural style of the prefabricated apartment blocks in the housing complexes around central Moscow was, perhaps, lacking in beauty.

The dramatic transformation that took place in the Russian life in recent years caused visible changes in the Moscow streets. Many Moscow neighborhoods can hardly be recognized now. In the last ten—twelve years many blocks of expensive apartments suddenly appeared all over central Moscow. Some upscale housing estates such as the "Alye Parusa" or the "Triumph Palace" can be regarded as modern architectural landmarks. Their architectural design is quite novel while their interiors are the ultimate in luxury.

In the new architectural epoch the city of Moscow also has managed to procure funds and to gather strength for reclaiming some of its holy places that had been destroyed in the recent past. The exact replica of the Christ the Savior Cathedral was built anew with the use of the original drawings and other historical materials. Hundreds of churches have been renovated and replicas of some of the destroyed churches and other historical buildings have been constructed. A park and a memorial complex dedicated to the Russian victory in the World War II was built. Dozens of new monuments were erected in the streets and squares of Moscow.

The history of a city cannot be reduced to merely the history of the relevant territory—it is the history of the culture associated with it. The values and

effects of culture do not age. The mighty and fast changes are constantly transforming the appearance of many Moscow districts and many Moscow suburbs. The nightly kaleidoscopically changing lights of specially designed illumination systems emphasize the elegance of the traditional Moscow architecture and the peculiarly outlined building of the most advanced styles. A.V. Ikonnikov, an eminent historian of the Russian architecture, once described the architectural image of Moscow as an "exciting spectacle". One tends to agree with the expert when looking at the new towering apartment blocks and public buildings of an intricately original design, the lovingly renovated ancient palaces, new parks, memorials, museums, entertainment centers, sports facilities, modern shopping arcades and many miles of new highways around Moscow. To see all that one just has to walk in the streets, lanes and squares around the center of Moscow or move away from the Kremlin walls along one on the ancient routes leading towards Saint Petersburg, and the old Russian cities of Yaroslavl, Ryazan, Nizhni Novgorod, and Kaluga.

The present album of photographs taken by Nikolai Rakhmanov is structured in exactly this arrangement taking the reader along the five routes. The photographer, an acclaimed chronicler of Moscow of the 20th century, is telling us about the fascinating transformations that keep on happening in Moscow.

The "exciting spectacle" is being continued.

Moscow International
Music House
and office center
"Kransnye Kholmy"

I

Red Square

Saint Basil Cathedral. 1555-1561. *Architects Barma and Postnik*
Memorial to Kuzma Minin and Prince Dmitry Pozharsky. 1804-1818. *Sculptor I.P. Martos*

Iconostasis of the Saint Basil Cathedral

Ivanovskaya Square and the Kremlin cathedrals *(pp. 16-17)*

Tsar Bell. 1733-1735. *Founders Ivan and Mikhail Motorin*

Tsar Cannon. 1586. *Cast by Andrey Chokhov*

Arkhangelsky Cathedral. 1505-1508. *Architect Aleviz Novy (pp. 20-21)*

Fragment of the icon "Archangel Mikhail". The early 15th century

Iconostasis of the Arkhangelsky Cathedral

22

Easter service at the portal of the Uspensky Cathedral *(pp. 24-25)*

Uspensky Cathedral. 1475-1479. *Architect Aristotle Fioravanti*

Iconostasis of the Uspensky Cathedral

Icon "The Virgin Hodigitria". Novgorod. 12th and 14th centuries

Icon "Saint George". Novgorod. 12th century

Tsar's place of Ivan the Terrible. 1551

28

Blagoveshchensky Cathedral. 1484-1489

Theophanes the Greek (?). Icons "Virgin" and "John the Baptist". End of the 14th century

Southern façade of the Teremnoy Palace. 1635-1636.
Architects Bazhen Ogurtsov, Trefil Sharutin, Larion Ushakov, Antip Konstantinov (pp. 32-33)

White stone ornamentation of the Throne Chamber

Golden (Red) Porch of the Teremnoy Palace

Council Chamber of the Teremnoy Palace *(pp. 36-37)*

———

Faceted Chamber. 1487-1491.
Architects Marko Fryazin, Pietro Antonio Solari

———

Main portal of the Faceted Chamber

———

Interior of the Faceted Chamber *(pp. 40-41)*

Great Kremlin Palace. 1838-1849. *Architect K.A. Ton*

A view of the Andreevsky Chamber in perspective

Georgievsky Chamber

Aleksandrovsky Chamber

Armory. 1844-1851. *Architect K.A. Ton*

Armory. Display of the Russian golden and silver articles of the 17th–the early 20th centuries

Armory. Displays of the West European arms and suits of armor of the 15th-19th centuries *(pp. 48-49)*

Summer carriage. 1770s. England. Gift of Count G. Orlov to the Empress Catherine the Great

Carriage. 1754. France. Gift of Count K.G. Razumovsky to the Empress Elizaveta Petrovna

Regalia of the Russian Empire. Hats and crowns of the Russian tsars and emperors

View of the Historical Museum and the Red Square (*pp. 52-53*)

The front entrance of the Historical Museum. Mural "The family tree of the Russian monarchs". 1883.
A group of artists headed by F.G. Toropov

Voskresenskie (Iverskie) Gate of Kitai Gorod. 1680. Replica built in 1995

Red Square. Upper shopping arcade (now called the State department store, or GUM). 1890-1893.
Architect A.N. Pomerantsev, engineer V.G. Shukhov

Fountain on the Manezhnaya Square.
Sculptor Z.K. Tsereteli (pp. 57-58)

View of the Manezhnaya Square from the Arsenalnaya Tower of the Kremlin

Manezhnaya Square (pp. 63-64)

———

Cast iron gate and railing of the Aleksandrovsky Garden.
Architect E. Pascal

———

Eternal Flame at the Tomb of Unknown Soldier in the Aleksandrovsky Garden

II

Bolshoy Theater. 1825, 1855-1856.
Architects O.I. Bove, A.A. Mikhailov, A.K. Kavos

Bolshoy Theater auditorium

New stage of the Bolshoy Theater

The house. View from the stalls

View of the Teatralnaya Square from the quadriga of the Bolshoy Theater. *Sculptor P.K. Klodt (pp. 72-73)*

Kamergersky Lane. Left: Moscow Art Theater

Tverskaya Street. Left: "National" hotel. 1903. *Architect A.I. Ivanov*

Memorial to A.S. Pushkin. 1880. *Sculptor A.M. Opekushin*

Tverskaya Street (*pp. 78-79*)

Tverskaya Square. Residence of the Mayor of Moscow

———

Nativity of Our Lady Church in Putinki. 1649-1652

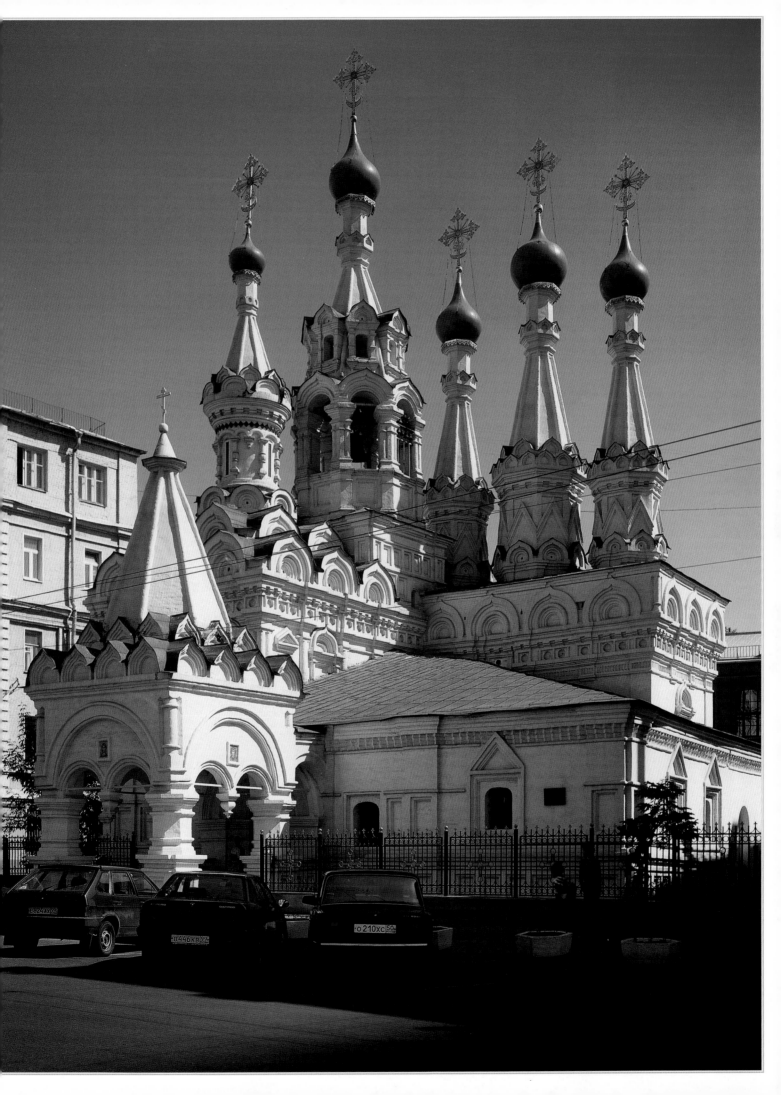

Museum of the Contemporary History of Russia (former English Club).
The late 18th—early 19th century

Metro station "Mayakovskaya". 1938.
Architect A.N. Dushkin. Artist A.A. Deineka. Awarded Grand Prix at the World Exhibition in New York

Metro station "Novoslobodskaya". 1952.
Architects A.N. Dushkin, A.F. Strelkov. Stained glass windows by artist P.D. Korin

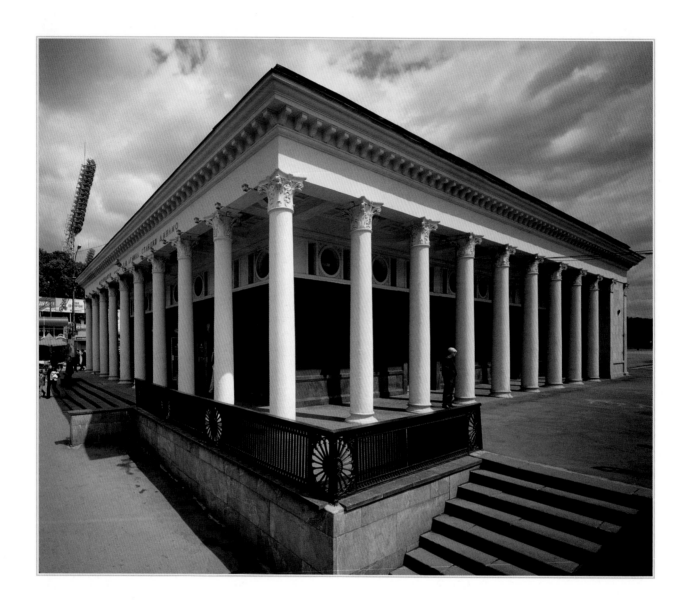

Metro station "Dynamo". Foyer. 1938.
Architect D.N. Chechulin

———

Northern River Port. 1937.
Architects A.M. Rukhlyadev, V.F. Krinsky

III

Tretyakovsky Passage Way

Memorial chapel to grenadiers who fought at the battle of Plevna. 1887.
Architect V.O. Shervud

———

Nikolskaya Street. Former Synod printing shop. 1811-1815.
Architect I.L. Mironovsky (pp. 92-93)

Metro station "Revolution Square". 1938.
Architect A.N. Dushkin. Sculptor M.G. Manizer

Komsomolskaya Square *(pp. 96-97)*

———

Kazansky Railway Station. 1913-1940.
Architect A.V. Shchusev

Yaroslavsky Railway Station. 1902-1904.
Architect F.O. Shekhtel

99

Metro station "Komsomolskaya-koltsevaya". 1952.
Architect A.V. Shchusev. Sculptors S. Kazakov, A. Sergeev.
Mosaic designs by artist P.D. Korin

———

Maiolica ceiling and wall murals in the metro station "Komsomolskaya".
Artist E.E. Lansere

Novaya Basmannaya Street. Fence railing of the 19th-century estate with the Peter and Paul Church in the background. 1705-1728 *(pp. 102-103)*

Watch tower of the Sokolniki fire-fighting station. 1881-1884

Epiphany Church in Elokhovo. 1835-1845. *Architect E.D. Tyurin*

Memorial "Conquerors of the Outer Space". 1964.
Sculptor A.P. Faidysh-Krandievsky. Architects M.O. Barshch, A.N. Kolchin

"Cosmos" hotel. 1976-1979. *Architects T.G. Zaikin, V.V. Steiskal*
Monument to Charles de Gaulle. 2005. *Sculptor Z.K. Tsereteli*

Central pavilion of the All-Russian Exhibition Center. 1954.
Architects V.G. Gelfreikh, V.A. Shchuko

———

Fountain the "Stone flower". 1954.
Architects K.G. Topuridze, G.D. Konstantinovsky

All-Russian Exhibition Center

IV

Romanovs Palace and the Znamensky Cathedral in the Varvarka Street

Church of Anna's Conception at the Zaryadye Corner. The early 16th century

Skyscraper apartment block on Kotelnicheskaya Embankment. 1952.
Architect D.N. Chechulin

———

Taganskaya Square

Andronikov Monastery. Established in 1357
———
Savior Cathedral of the Andronikov Monastery. 1420-1427

Resurrection Church in the Kadashi quarter. 1687-1713. *Architect S. Turchaninov*

Saint Nikolai Church on Bersenevka. 1656-1657

Front façade of the Tretyakov Gallery. 1900-1905. *Design by artist V.M. Vasnetsov*
Memorial to P.M. Tretyakov. 1980. *Sculptor A.P. Kibalnikov*

Christ the Savior. Second half of the 12th century. Novgorod

Theophanes the Greek (?). Our Lady of Don. 1380-1390

Tretyakov Gallery. Room of ancient Russian paintings (icons)

Tretyakov Gallery. Room of paintings by Aleksandr Ivanov.
The canvas "Christ coming to people" is at the center

Saint Daniel Monastery. Established in the late 13th century
by the Moscow Prince Daniel Aleksandrovich *(pp. 128-129)*

Panorama of the Kolomenskoe estate

Ascension Church on the Kolomenskoe estate. 1532 *(left)*

Our Lady of Kazan Church. 1660s

Tsaritsino. Architectural and park ensemble in the neo-Gothic style.
Architects V.I. Bazhenov, M.F. Kazakov.
Figure gate. 1780s

Tsaritsino. Fancy bridge. 1780s

Kuskovo park and palace estate.
Park. Large conservatory in the background. 1761-1763.
Architects D. Antonov, F.S. Argunov (top left)

———

Grotto pavilion. 1756-1775. *Architect F.S. Argunov*

———

Manor house. 1769-1775. *Architect K.I. Blank*

V

Christ the Savior Cathedral. 1839-1883.
Architect K.A. Ton. Replica built in the 1990s

———

Interior of the Christ the Savior Cathedral

Pashkov House. 1784-1788. *Architect V.I. Bazhenov (?)*

Pushkin Fine Arts Museum. 1898-1912. *Architect R.I. Klein*

Pushkin Fine Arts Museum. Italian courtyard

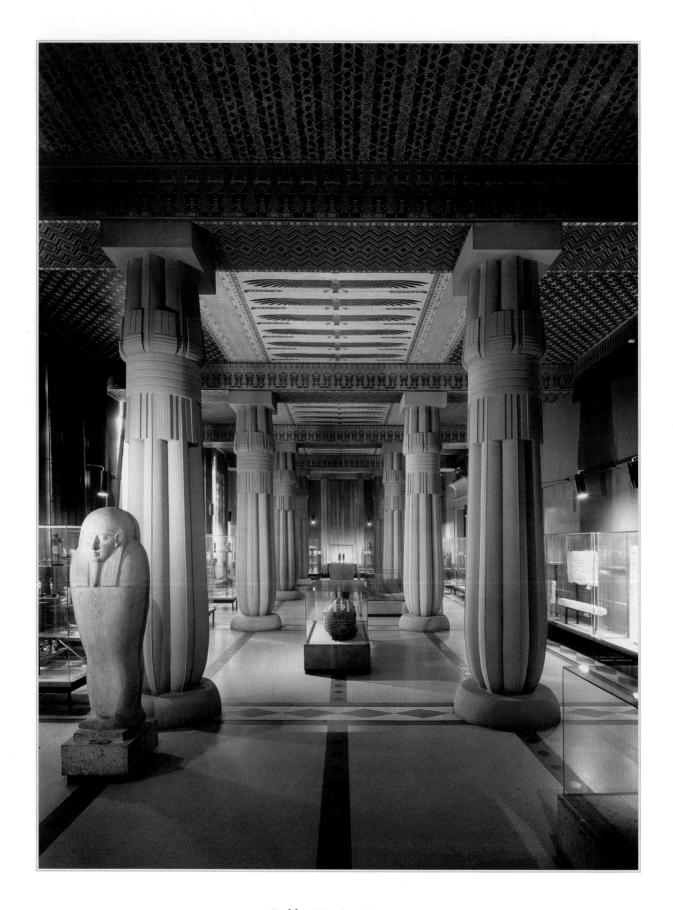

Pushkin Fine Arts Museum.
Room of ancient Egyptian art

Art gallery halls

View of the Krymsky Bridge and Christ the Savior Cathedral
from the Neskuchny Garden *(pp. 148-149)*

Novodevichy (Our Lady of Smolensk) Nunnery.
Established in 1524

Luzhniki sports complex panorama

Memorial to the first man in space on Gagarin Square. 1980. *Sculptor P.I. Bondarenko*

———

Transgaz office block on the Kaluzhskoe Highway

———

Moscow State University, Vorobievy Gory. 1949-1953.
Architects L.V. Rudnev, S.E. Chernyshev, V.N. Nasonov, A.F. Khryakov (pp. 156-157)

VI

Russian State Library.
Memorial to Fedor Dostoevsky. 1998. *Sculptor A.I. Rukavishnikov*

———

Arbat Square *(top right)*

———

"Prague" restaurant at the "confluence" of the Arbat Street and New Arbat

Arbat Street *(pp. 162-163)*

———

Arbat. Vakhtangov Theater and the "Turandot" fountain

———

Memorial to Bulat Okudzhava, the poet of Arbat. 2002.
Sculptor G.V. Frangulyan

Town house in Denezhny Lane
(Manor house of A.K. Polivanov). 1822-1823 *(pp. 166-167)*

State Pushkin Museum. 1814.
Architect A.G. Grigoriev. Sculptor I.P. Vitali

Interiors of the State Pushkin Museum

Ministry of Foreign Affairs in the Smolenskaya Square. 1948-1953.
Architects V.G. Gelfreikh, M.A. Minkus

Europe Square at the Kievsky Railway Station. "Abduction of Europe" fountain. 2002.
Sculptor Olivier Stroebel (Belgium)

Kievsky Railway Station. 1912-1917. *Architect I.I. Rerberg*

———

Footbridge near the Kievsky Railway Station. 2002.
Architect Yu.P. Platonov (top right)

———

Footbridge "Bagration". 1997. *Architect B. Tkhor*

———

Borodinsky Bridge. 1912. *Architect R.I. Klein.*
Russian Government building in the background *(pp. 174-175)*

Metro station "Kievskaya-koltsevaya". 1954.
Architects E.I. Katonin, V.K. Skugarev. Mosaic designs by artist A.V. Mizin

Three epochs of the Moscow architecture

In the Moscow Zoo

Victory Square. Triumphal Arch. 1827-1834.
Architect O.I. Bove. Sculptor I.P. Vitali. Replica built in the 1960s

———

Memorial to the Victory in the Great Patriotic War of 1941-1945 on Poklonnaya Gora. 1983-1995.
Architects A.T. Polyansky, L.V. Vavakin. Sculptor Z.K. Tsereteli

MOSCOW

Photographs by
NIKOLAI RAKHMANOV

———

Альбом на английском языке

Interbook Business Publishers
Russia, 123104, Moscow, Spiridonievsky per., 12/9, office 12
Phone: (495) 956-13-92, 200-64-62; fax: (495) 956-37-52
E-mail: info@interbook-art.ru; www. interbook-art.ru